Coffee With God

31 Day Prayer Devotional for Wives

CHARITY R. DEAN

Copyright © 2016 Charity R. Dean

Cover design: Destiny House Publishing, LLC

Artwork: Can Stock Photo

Photo credits: Monique Styles

All rights reserved.

Destiny House Publishing, LLC
P.O. Box 19774 Detroit, MI 48219
www.destinyhousepublishing.com

ISBN: 1936867257
ISBN-13: 978-1-936867-25-7

DEDICATIONS

To the wives that have joined me for coffee: Ra'Sheedah Debose, Pamela Gary, LaWanda Montgonery, LaQuitia Robinson, Aries Winans, and Ticie Winans,

To my "babies", who will be wives one day: Kristin D'Ashley, Taylor Blackston, Jasmine Carter, Gabby Clark, Cristy Miles, LaShara Montgomery, Jocelyn Sample, Lauren Tillman and Dannah Wilson,

To all wives and engaged women around the world

May your mornings and evenings be filled with time for coffee (and tea and cocoa) with God.

CHARITY DEAN

There is something about morning time with God. I have experienced awesome time with the Lord in the early moments of the day. Our ritual is simple. I wake up, go in the kitchen and brew some coffee. I, then, grab my Bible, prayer journal, pen, and cup of Joe and sit and chat with my King. It's a wonderful experience.

I believe that the Lord wants that quality time with each and every one of his children. As I began to work on this prayer journal, it changed from being for his children, to for his daughters, and from being for his daughters to being for his married (and engaged) daughters.

So I pray this journal will minister to you and your marriage the way writing it has done for me. I pray that every wife and future wife that reads this will experience freshness in her reliance on the LORD. May God catapult your relationship with Him and may he do a supernatural work on your husbands.

I love you.

Charity R. Dean

CONTENTS

Acknowledgments	Pg 8
Day One	Pg 9
Day Two	Pg 13
Day Three	Pg 17
Day Four	Pg 21
Day Five	Pg 25
Day Six	Pg 29
Day Seven	Pg 33
Day Eight	Pg 37
Day Nine	Pg 41
Day Ten	Pg 45
Day Eleven	Pg 49
Day Twelve	Pg 53
Day Thirteen	Pg 57
Day Fourteen	Pg 61
Day Fifteen	Pg 65
Day Sixteen	Pg 69
Day Seventeen	Pg 73

CONTENTS continued

Day Eighteen	Pg 77
Day Nineteen	Pg 81
Day Twenty	Pg 85
Day Twenty-one	Pg 89
Day Twenty-two	Pg 93
Day Twenty-three	Pg 97
Day Twenty-four	Pg 101
Day Twenty-five	Pg 105
Day Twenty-six	Pg 109
Day Twenty-seven	Pg 113
Day Twenty-eight	Pg 117
Day Twenty-nine	Pg 121
Day Thirty	Pg 125
Day Thirty-one	Pg 129

ACKNOWLEDGMENTS

My favorite coffee partner, my Lord and Savior, Jesus Christ. Thank you for everything.

My best friend forever and my muse, Erik Anderson Dean

My parents and examples in ministry and in life, Apostle Oscar and Prophetess Crystal Jones

My parents-in-love and always in support, John and Norma Dean

My mentor, LaVonne Thomas (although she doesn't do coffee)

Pastors John and Minnie Hardy, planters of numerous seeds of wisdom into my marriage and my life

My siblings Jake and Keila Allen, Kyria Jones, Kelly Dean, LaTina Jones, and Christopher Jones.

My niece & goddaughter, Arielle Jones

DAY ONE

"And the Lord plagued Pharoah and his house with great plagues because of Sarai, Abram's house." Genesis 12: 17

God had just called Abram and given him blessings. He told him that he would make a great nation out of him, that he would bless him and make his name great. But Abram had a faith problem. He heard God and even obeyed him. He began to move out of his home country as God commanded. However, Abram was not completely convinced. When he arrived in Egypt, he was afraid that he would be killed, so he made his wife pretend to be his sister. As a result, Sarai was taken into Pharaoh's home and Abram was given many things in exchange for his bride.

The Bible does not show Sarai's emotions during this time. I imagine that she went through a variety of emotions. This man of strength and faith, her husband, all of a sudden became weakened and timid.

She believed him when he said that God said move. She believed him when he said that God said He would bless those that blessed him and curse those that cursed him. But here he was, the man that caused them to leave everything they knew to follow his God, and now he was scheming and plotting out of fear. They had just left the place of Bethel, where Abram had built an altar for God. And now her husband is asking her to do the unthinkable. And Sarai did it. She was taken into the house of Pharaoh. Her husband gave her to another man, because he was afraid for his life. God has called us to be submissive to our husbands. But God was NOT happy with this situation. Sarai was his daughter. She belonged to Him. Just as God had a promise and purpose for Abram, he had one for Sarai as well. Abram's actions did not please God.

However Sarai did not leave Abram in his moment of weakness. When our husbands, succumb to fear and doubt, or ego and pride, God is not pleased, he will not leave his daughters to suffer at the hands of his disobedient sons.

Even when it seems that God is not moving in an unresponsive husband, he does not sit back and watch his daughters get mistreated. The Lord began to plague Pharaoh's entire household until his daughter was back in her rightful place with her husband.

When you are experiencing difficulty with your husband, don't immediately give up. God loves you. He will not leave you or forsake you. Have you ever felt like Sarai? What happened?

Read Genesis 12 and talk to God about how that relates to you. Record your thoughts.

_____
_____
_____
_____
_____
_____
_____
_____
_____
_____
_____
_____

COFFEE WITH GOD

CHARITY DEAN

DAY TWO

"And his mother said unto him, Upon me be thy curse, my son: only obey my voice, and go fetch me them" Genesis 27: 13

Giving birth is one of the most powerful experiences on this earth. Men will never understand what it means to carry a child for nine months and then push a beautiful human being out of your body. It's truly a spiritual experience.

However, no matter how moving it is, there is truly balance in everything. Our children do not belong to us. They belong to God. Sometimes for a variety of reasons, maybe because we wanted a baby so bad, or because we just wanted to be loved by a baby, we place our children on a pedestal before husbands; and even sometimes before God. This is not the order of God and it is not beneficial for the children or for you as a mother.

Rebekah, interfered with the plan of God, because she favored one son over the other. Her obsession with Jacob caused her to trick her husband into giving Jacob, Esau's blessing. She was willing to not only manipulate her husband for Jacob but she said, "upon me be thy curse."

Her "love" was a worldly love. Worldly love is selfish. It says to put your child above your husband. Give your child whatever they want. We have raised a generation of spoiled, bratty children with short attention spans and large entitlement issues. God calls us to love our children like He loves us. The Bible says He chastens those whom He loves. Rebekah's dysfunctional love for her son caused both of her sons to suffer.

To love children as God loves, we must learn about God's love. How are you parenting? What ways can you improve your love relationship with your child(ren)?

_____
_____
_____
_____
_____
_____
_____
_____
_____
_____
_____
_____
_____
_____
_____
_____
_____
_____
_____
_____
_____
_____
_____
_____
_____
_____
_____

COFFEE WITH GOD

DAY THREE

"And Miriam the prophetess, the sister of Aaron, took a timbrel in her hand; and all the women when out after her with timbrels and dance"   Exodus 15:20

Miriam was Moses's sister. She was a leader among the people. After God delivered the Israelites from the hand of Pharaoh, the women looked to Miriam for leadership. When she began to worship the lord, all the other women began to worship. Sometimes our obedience and reverence to God becomes infectious and causes other women to praise and worship God. That is why it is so important to give God glory.

One might think, that since all the women were rescued, they would all naturally begin to praise and worship God. However, sometimes people aren't aware that praise and worship are natural responses to the goodness of God. Maybe they are busy caught up in the next "trial". Or maybe they don't realize the magnitude of what God has done.

Often times, when I talk to wives who are frustrated with their husband's spiritual place, I ask them if he has made ANY progress at all. The answer is usually yes. Perhaps he is not moving fast enough. That is a dangerous place for a wife to be. We should never stand by after God has done a miracle. We should be so in tuned with God that every miracle gets a praise. And like Miriam, our response to God's greatness can cause other women to worship as well.

What are some miracles God has performed in your marriage? Have you shared that testimony with others? How can you inspire more women to praise?

_____

COFFEE WITH GOD

DAY FOUR

"And Miriam and Aaron spake against Moses because of the Ethopian woman whom he had married for he married an Ethopian woman" Numbers 12:1

Here we see this leader, Miriam, again. This time she is speaking against *her* leader, Moses. There is a saying, "hurting people hurt people." This phrase goes further, and studies have proven that 'oppressed people oppress people' and 'rejected people reject people'. It is a cycle of viciousness common to the human race. The only way to stop this cycle, is through the power of forgiveness.

Miriam looked down on her sister-in-law because of her ethnicity. Not many years prior, Miriam was a slave because of her ethnicity.

As Christians, we must live a lifestyle of forgiveness. When we don't forgive, we set the stage to repeat the very harm that was done to us. Forgiveness is not an option for the Christian wife. It is a lifestyle. We must commit to forgiving our pastors, leaders, husbands, and children daily. If not, the same offense that infected us, we will infect someone else. Instead of being the offended , we become the offender; in need of the same forgiveness we are withholding. Break the vicious cycle in your life by choosing to forgive.

What is the one thing that hurts every time you bring it up? Where do you need to practice forgiveness? Write it down. Be honest with the Lord about how that makes you feel. Then forgive. Release the offense and the offender.

COFFEE WITH GOD

DAY FIVE

But the word is very nigh unto thee, in thy mouth, and in thy heart, that thou mayest do it. Deuteronomy 30:14

Women fill church pews more plentiful than men. We flock to women's retreats and conferences, praying for a word from the Lord. And when the speaker says something that directly relates to our situation, we rejoice in God's rhema, "on time" message. We rejoice even more when we hear a prophetic word tailor fit for us. It encourages us, increases our faith and reminds us that God is concerned about the things that concern us. What an amazing feeling! However, as women of God, God wants more from us. He wants to speak directly to us and often times, He is. We are just so busy or afraid that we "can't" hear from Him, that we don't take the time to stop and listen.

There is no magical formula that separates the prophet from us. There is no school or training needed to hear a Word from God. If you have a relationship with God, he is talking to you. The question is, are you listening? I have often experienced that when I sit still and ask the Lord to speak to me, He does. It is really that simple. Even as you read this, the Lord has a Word for you. Stop and listen. What is he saying?

_____
_____
_____
_____
_____
_____
_____

COFFEE WITH GOD

DAY SIX

Therefore we said, Let us now prepare to build us an altar, not for burnt offering, nor sacrifice: But that it may be a witness between us, and you, and our generations after us, that we might do the service of the LORD before him with our burnt offerings and with our sacrifices, and with our peace offerings; that your children may not say to our children in time to come, Ye have no part in the LORD Joshua 22:26-27

As a wife, your actions teach your daughters how to behave and your sons what to look for in a wife. Your children learn not only from how you interact with your spouse but from the things you teach them.

I will never forget having family devotions as a child, or our daily family prayer in the car growing up. Now that I have my own family, those things help shape what legacy I want to leave with my children. My husband and I do things a bit differently, but it is important for us to lay a foundation of prayer and family in our children's lives. Every family will not look the same.

What are some ways that you and your husband honor the Lord as a couple? What are some traditions you have as a family? What are some things you want to improve?

_____
_____
_____
_____
_____

COFFEE WITH GOD

DAY SEVEN

But if serving the LORD seems undesirable to you, then choose for yourselves this day whom you will serve, whether the gods your ancestors served beyond the Euphrates, or the gods of the Amorites, in whose land you are living. But as for me and my house,, we will serve the LORD." Joshua 24:15

This scripture is a reminder that serving God is a choice. Here, Joshua was telling the people that it was up to them how they would proceed. The famous verse "as for me and my household..." is often used in sermons about families. But there is a more personal approach to this scripture.

Serving God means loving Him enough to do as He commands us in His word, even when it seems undesirable. Serving God is a choice that we can't necessarily make for anyone other than ourselves. We can't force our husbands or even our children to serve God. It is fruitless to nag your spouse into prayer, devotion, or some other type of service. However, we can serve God for ourselves and allow our example to impact those closest to us.

In what ways can you serve God more? Do you find yourself trying to make that choice for your husband? In what ways can you focus on yourself and serve God and others better?

_____
_____
_____
_____
_____

COFFEE WITH GOD

DAY EIGHT

But his wife said unto him, If the LORD were pleased to kill us, he would not have received a burnt offering and a meat offering at our hands, neither would have shewed us all these things, nor would as at the time have told us such as these"
Judges 13:23

I encourage you to grab a Bible and read the entire 13th chapter of Judges. There Monoah and his wife had an experience with an angel. After the angel told Monoah and his barren wife that they would have a child, Monoah offered a burnt offering to God. The flames went up from the alter and the angle ascended into heaven with the flames. Monoah was astounded and said, "We have seen God, we will surely die". His response is interesting because it is as if he forgets everything that transpired before the offering. He and his wife had been praying for years for a child and God finally answers their prayer. God sends an angel to give specific instructions. And yet, Monoah is only focused on what is before him at that moment. As the leader of the house, often men can be easily short-sighted, only focused on the thing in front of them. As wives, it is our responsibility when we see our husbands in that place, to remind them of the goodness of God and his promise for our family. This means in order for us to be in our proper place, we must be operating from a place of faith. You can't remind and encourage when you are not convinced yourself. We must believe that what God said to us and concerning our family is true. Then we have to encourage our husbands. Men carry such huge burdens as the head of the family and often times they can only see what is in front of them because they are in "protector/provider" mode. It is not because they don't have a relationship with God, but it is because they are trying to care for their families. We operate best as a team. And when we are fully operational as a team, we are sure to give birth to the promise. Here Monoah's wife reminded him of God's promises and the next verse says "So the woman gave birth to a boy and named him Samson". Notice that Monoah's wife was not passively sitting by nor did she admonish him and tear him down with her words. Her response was simple. She reminded him of God's promise.

What promises has God made to you? How do you remind your husband of those promises?

_____
_____
_____
_____
_____
_____
_____
_____
_____
_____
_____
_____
_____
_____
_____
_____
_____
_____

COFFEE WITH GOD

DAY NINE

"And she went down unto the floor, and did according to all that her mother in law bade her." Ruth 3:6

Ruth was an extraordinary woman. One of the numerous ways in which I am fascinated by her, is her deep love relationship with her mother-in-law. Ruth didn't just "tolerate" her mother-in-law. But she loved her as if she were her biological mother. She served her with sincerity.

For a myriad of reasons, it is so easy to come in competition with your husband's mother. Usually, she is the most important lady in our guy's life before our arrival. She gave birth to him and is the first woman to ever love him. It can be intimidating. The mother-in-law/daughter-in-law relationship is one that requires tenderness, prayer, wisdom and humility. If you disregard your mother-in-law and do not invest in your relationship with her, you are not only doing a disservice to yourself but also to your husband.

Every relationship will be different. For some people it will be very easy to have a good relationship with their mother-in-law. For some it will be very difficult. However, the instruction for all of us is the same, we must honor our mothers. The wise wife will not only honor her, but she will invest in her own relationship with her mother-in-law. She will serve her mother-in-law as if she was her birth mother. And she will reap the benefits of such a relationship.

How would you describe your relationship with your mother in law? What are ways that it can improve? What are 5 things you will do this month to improve your relationship with her?

___

COFFEE WITH GOD

DAY TEN

"And David said to Abigail, Blessed be the LORD God of Israel, which sent thee this day to meet me" **I Samuel 25:32**

If you have the time, please read the entire 25th chapter of I Samuel. Abigail's husband who was a wise business man made a foolish decision. His pride stepped in the way and her household was in danger. Abigail knew what her husband had done and she moved quickly. She gathered items in her house to present to the future king as an offering to cover her husband's unwise choices. Abigail was brave. She went directly to David and began to make a case for her family. She was influential and persuasive. As a result, she saved her entire house, including her foolish husband. Abigail was prudent enough to respond when her house was in trouble. She immediately went into action, and then she humbled herself at David's feet. His response was to call her blessed.

What do you do when your house is in trouble? Do you play the blame game? Nowhere in the chapter does Abigail run to her husband and yell at him because of their impending doom. She recognized her place as an equal team member and immediately acted on behalf of her family. Humility and presenting an offering were the immediate ways that she was able to persuade David not to harm her family.

Ask God how you can help your family today? Do you value your role as an equal team member? In what ways do you need to go to the King on your family's behalf? Take time right now to pray about what struggles may be facing your household. See yourself as an equal team player and go into action. Talk to the King. When you do that, you are blessed.

_____
_____
_____
_____
_____
_____
_____
_____
_____
_____
_____
_____
_____
_____
_____
_____
_____
_____
_____
_____
_____
_____
_____
_____
_____
_____
_____
_____

COFFEE WITH GOD

DAY ELEVEN

"The Lord is my rock and my fortress and my deliverer; The God of my strength, in whom I trust; My shield." 2 Samuel 22:2-3

After the Lord delivered David from his enemies, he wrote and sang this song to the Lord. He described God as his fortress. In a time of war, a fortress is a source of protection for battle worn soldiers. Webster's Dictionary describes a fortress as "impenetrable."

Marriage inevitably comes with battles. Some harder than others, some more complex than others. Some marriages are losing the battle because miscommunication, financial distress, and/or infidelity. When we face those battles, God wants to be our fortress. He is our safe place where we can rest. When we run to Him, we can rest knowing that He is an impenetrable resting place. When we are safe in His arms, we can get direction and instructions to face the battles that are inevitable to marriage.

What battles are you currently facing? What is your strategy for your battle? God wants to be your safe place. Spend some time talking to Him about the battles you are facing. Let Him give you instruction.

_____
_____
_____
_____
_____

COFFEE WITH GOD

DAY TWELVE

Arise, get thee to Zarephath, which belongeth to Zidon, and dwell there: behold, I have commanded a widow woman there to sustain thee. I Kings 17:9

These are the words that the Lord spoke to Elijah. Elijah had been hiding in the Kerith Ravine. God had told him to go there and while he was there Elijah drank from the brook and ravens brought him food. Elijah stayed there for a while. Eventually the brook dried up because there was no rain. Then the Lord told him to go to a new place where He had told a widow woman to take care of him.

I imagine that Elijah had a great amount of faith. He had spent much time alone, receiving his nourishment directly from God. Now, it was time for Elijah to go to a new place and receive help from someone else. God would use a widow to help him. Widows are mentioned throughout the Bible. Often times, God commands us to take care of widows. Here, God is doing something different. He has commanded the widow to take care of the man of God.

As wives, how do we respond to help? How should we respond? Many women become so used to helping others that we don't know how to respond to help, especially when it comes from someone we think needs our help. Sometimes we even reject help based on who it comes from. God wants us to be humble enough to receive help. He commanded the widow to help Elijah.

If Elijah had been prideful and refused the help, it is likely that the widow and her son would have died (read the rest of the chapter). It wasn't just about Elijah andt is not always about us.

Has someone offered help to you? How do you respond? In what ways can you be more open to help?

_____
_____
_____
_____
_____
_____
_____
_____
_____
_____
_____
_____
_____
_____
_____
_____
_____
_____
_____
_____
_____
_____
_____
_____
_____

COFFEE WITH GOD

DAY THIRTEEN

The king asked the woman, and she told him about it. Then the king chose an officer to help her. "Give the woman everything that is hers," the king said. "Give her all the money made from her land from the day she left until now." II Kings 8:6

Hard times are inevitable. How we respond to hard times are what separate the strong from the weak, the wise from the not-so wise. This woman had fallen on really hard times. God had shown his strength to the woman already. Her son had died and through his prophet Elisha, he had been made alive again. Almost immediately, however, Elisha told her that a famine was coming over the land and she had to leave. I imagine the range of emotions that this woman had to experience.

Had God saved her son only so that they would lose everything and starve to death? Surely not. But she was at a crossroad. And she chose to trust the God that had proven He was in charge. She left her land for seven years. What faith! When she returned, God restored everything she lost. Hard times are inevitable. Trusting God despite the way things look, despite how we feel in hard times is what makes us wise women. It would do us well to remember our husbands and children are watching our response. Our actions can leave a much more lasting impact than our words. When we demonstrate a life of faith and trust in God especially when things are hard, we show our families how good God is and He is sure to prove himself over and over.

What hard times have you faced recently? How did you respond? Have you had any teachable moments throughout it?

COFFEE WITH GOD

CHARITY DEAN

DAY FOURTEEN

" Go and get all the Jewish people in Susa together. For my sake, giving up eating ; do not eat or drink for three days, night and day. I and my servant girls will also give up eating. Then I will go to the king, even though it is against the law, and if I die, I die." Esther 4:16

No pressure, right? Esther is one of my favorite women in the Bible. She is a superhero. She is brave. As a Jewish orphan, I am sure she was just excited to be considered as a candidate for queen. And then to be selected to be the queen! I can only imagine her excitement and joy. What an honor!

It was a short-lived excitement as her people were in danger. God places us in various positions for a reason. It is not so that we can be self-pleased with "how far we have come". The greatest leaders in history stand out to us because they used their positions of power and influence to impact the world; to make a difference. Often times, that comes with great risk. Martin Luther King was targeted by the Federal Government, Harriet Tubman was free but turned back to bring many other slaves to freedom placing her own life in danger. Esther, could have been killed for going to the King when he didn't call, especially to then ask for mercy for the Jews. But she didn't care. Esther was chosen to be queen for this purpose and so on she went. Esther was strategic, however. She planned a strategy to achieve victory. She was confident in the skills and beauty that God had given her. She organized a group to pray and fast on her behalf and she executed the plan flawlessly. Have you been called to do something that puts something at risk? In what positions has God strategically placed you? Take some time now to evaluate where you are. Why are you there? What turmoil surrounds you that you are called to fix? Ask God for wisdom and strategy.

_____
_____
_____
_____
_____
_____
_____
_____
_____
_____
_____
_____
_____
_____
_____
_____
_____
_____
_____
_____
_____
_____
_____
_____

COFFEE WITH GOD

DAY FIFTEEN

I cry out to the Lord; I pray to the Lord for mercy. I pour out my problems to him; I tell him my troubles. When I'm afraid, you Lord, know the way out. Psalms 142:1-3

Where do you turn when you are distressed? Who do you call? Your mother? Your sister? Your best friend? Don't get me wrong, relationships are important and certainly they have their place. However as a married (or soon to be married) woman, we must use wisdom when we go through trying times.

First, sharing too much can backfire especially if you husband is not in agreement with who you choose share information. Secondly, you have be careful because sharing everything opens the door for opinions that don't always leave once the issue is resolved. There are definitely other consequences that arise when you share everything with everyone. One of the biggest issues is that when we run to mom or our girlfriends whenever trouble hits, we essentially put them in a place where God should be. The psalmist in the above verse says he goes to God when there is trouble. That should be our first response. God is the only one that can change our situation and we should not leave until after we have exhausted all of our options. He should be first. Now, there is for sure wisdom through friends and mentors. By no means am I suggesting that we go through things without others. The suggestion is more about priority - God first. When we come to him, he can give us wisdom about what our next steps are and who they involve. That order is always the most important. What issues have you discussed with others? Have you sought God about them? Take time now to do that. What he is saying to you?

COFFEE WITH GOD

DAY SIXTEEN

"Don't forget your friend or your parent's friend. Don't always go to your family for help when trouble comes. A neighbor close by is better than a family far away." Proverbs 27:10

This scripture reminds us that friendships are important to God. It is also a reminder on how to deal with marital issues. Often times, when we have a spat with our spouse, we are tempted to call a mom or a sister. They have known us all our lives and they would understand. But this method it not always wise. Your family will hear and often times they will not forget. It is best to have a trusted friend (one that your spouse trusts as well) that you can talk to when things are rough. This friend will be able to hear you, give wisdom, and support your marriage. In order to have friends like this, you must be that type of friend for others.

Take some time and evaluate your friendships. What type of friends do you have? What can you do to be a better friend? Do you stand on your friend's side or on the side of the marriage?

_____
_____
_____
_____
_____
_____
_____
_____
_____
_____

COFFEE WITH GOD

DAY SEVENTEEN

Who can find a virtuous wife? For her worth is far above rubies. Proverbs 31:10

One of the most noteworthy scripture passages regarding women is Proverbs 31. This passage describes the characteristics of a virtuous wife. The chapter opens not by setting out a list of do's and don'ts. It opens by describing her worth. Having not found something that has more worth than a virtuous wife, the author likens the wife to possibly the most valuable stone he knows. And then he says she far surpasses those stones- rubies. What a beautiful reminder!

As wives, it easy to get lost in our responsibilities and obligations. Too often, society measures us by what we do or don't do. But this passage is a simple, yet refreshing, reminder. God does not measure our worth by what we do. He doesn't measure our worth by what we don't do. We are simply valuable as we are. Take some time today and take off the burdens placed on you by people or even yourself. Take off the responsibilities and obligations. Turn on some worship music and rest. What does it mean to you that your worth is not predicated on what you do? Do you struggle in this area?

_____
_____
_____
_____
_____
_____
_____

COFFEE WITH GOD

DAY EIGHTEEN

The LORD says, "Even now, come back to me with all your heart. Go without food, and cry and be sad. Let your heart be broken. Come back to the LORD your God, because he is kind and shows mercy. He doesn't become angry quickly, and he has great love. He can change his mind about doing harm. Joel 2:12-13

Humans sin. Wives sin. Sometimes we sin on purpose. As wives, we can sin in lots of areas: unfaithfulness (in heart and action), anger, self-righteousness, bitterness, gossip, unforgiveness and the list goes on. Sin separates us from God. The distance impacts our ability to hear from God and clouds our judgment. Sin also leads to shame. It causes us to further the distance between us and God because we are ashamed of what we have done.

But there is great news. God is never surprised at our sin. He knows before we sin and yet He loves us and forgives us the moment we repent. This scripture in Joel is about repentance. The message here is that you will sin. It is an inevitable part of our humanity. That said, we don't have to stay there. We should come back to God completely. When we return to Him, we should be truly sorry. He will always forgive us and welcome him back into His arms.

Today, evaluate your life. Have you been unfaithful in your heart, actions or words? Are there other areas of sin in your life? Write them down. Confess to God. Repent. Take time to reflect on how your actions will be different so that you can show you are truly sorry.

COFFEE WITH GOD

DAY NINETEEN

Though one may be overpowered, two can defend themselves. A cord of three strands is not quickly broken. **Ecclesiastes 4:12**

At our wedding, we had a ceremony where we tied together a three-fold chord while this verse was read. At that time, I understood the meaning of the verse and the symbolism for our marriage. It meant that while Erik and I made a great team, we were unbreakable with God in the mix. It now has so much more relevance. I have experienced firsthand the impact my relationship with God has had on my marriage. When I am intentional about serving God, inevitably my marriage is impacted for the better. When I am distant from God, inevitably my marriage suffers. A relationship with God and desire to seek him regularly leads us to focus on being His servants in this earth. This is a selfless experience that trickles into our closest relationships, especially our husbands. The reverse happens as well. When we are less focused on God, we are more focused on ourselves, and our actions are self-focused instead of God-focused. That also impacts the marriage. When God is intentionally in the relationship, both parties can focus on God and inevitably lead a life of serving Him, which means serving others. It is a true win-win- win situation.

What role does God play in your marriage? What practical ways can you improve on your relationship with God?

_____
_____
_____
_____
_____

COFFEE WITH GOD

DAY TWENTY

Jesus turned and saw the woman and said, "Be encouraged dear woman. You are made well because you believed." Matthew 9: 22

I think we often underestimate the power of faith. In this passage, a woman had been sick for very many years. She had set her mind to becoming healed. She believed that if she would touch Jesus' garments she would be healed. She had heard of miracles and knew without doubt that she could be a recipient of his miracle-working power. And so she set out to see Jesus. She touched him and was healed. Jesus spoke to her. I think he wanted to clarify something to her and to us. She didn't need to physically touch him to be healed. He wanted her to truly understand the power of faith. For He knew He was going to be crucified. He would not always be present in the flesh. He told her "It was your faith that healed you". How powerful is that?! We don't need to physically touch Jesus to be healed, changed, or delivered. Our faith is enough.

What are we waiting for to "touch Jesus"? If Jesus was present in the flesh, what would we take to him for healing? Spend your time in prayer today about that thing. Increase your faith in that area. Your faith is what will make you whole.

_____
_____
_____
_____
_____

COFFEE WITH GOD

DAY TWENTY-ONE

Jesus answered, "Moses allowed you to divorce your wives because you refused to accept God's teaching, but divorce was not allowed in the beginning." Matthew 19:8

There were two couples that were on two different islands. The first couple saw a broken boat nearby. That couple enjoyed the island. But whenever they got bored or argued, they would glance at that boat. When there was a really bad argument one of them would even sleep on the boat. One day after spending the night on the boat, the wife realized that the broken boat just needed a couple of touches and it would be fixed. Eventually she fixed the boat. And after the next argument, she was gone.

The second couple had the same struggles as the first couple. They argued just as much. They also had a broken boat nearby. However, when they got bored they got creative by using the resources they found on the island. They used the wood from the broken boat to create a fire. After an argument, they would cuddle by the fire and talk over their differences. This couple lived on this island together for their entire lives.

The boat represents divorce. If you removed divorce as an option, it will never be an option. It's that simple. When you have a way out, eventually you will use that way of escape. However, the couples that eliminate divorce as an option, have no other choice but to work out their differences. Jesus tells us that divorce is not in his original plan. Make a decision today that your marriage will be lived according to his plan.

COFFEE WITH GOD

DAY TWENTY-TWO

This woman did the only thing she could do for me; she poured perfume on my body to prepare me for burial Mark 14:8

Jesus is sitting with his disciples and a woman comes into the room with expensive perfume and anoints his feet with it. She is subject to whispers and ridicule as she makes her way through the room. But she does not care. She has a gift for her king. It was the perfect gift. Jesus was about to be crucified. Her gift to him was not only sacrificial but it was symbolic. How do you give a gift to the One that is a gift? This perfume cost this woman something. It was not cheap. Even walking into the room to place it on the feet of Jesus cost her embarrassment and shame- but she was intent on giving her gift to Jesus.

As a wife, what gift can we give to Jesus? Something that is costly and sacrificial? We can give our marriage to Him. We give our marriages to Christ when we submit to His will. We give our marriage to Christ when we honor our husbands. We give our marriages to Christ , when despite what society says, we eliminate divorce as an option. Today, we are invited to do the "only thing we can do for Him"- surrender. Let's give Him our marriage today.

_____
_____
_____
_____
_____
_____
_____

CHARITY DEAN

COFFEE WITH GOD

DAY TWENTY-THREE

And when the daughter of the said Herodias came in, and danced, and pleased Herod and them that sat with him, the king said unto the damsel, Ask of me whatsoever thou wilt, and I will give it thee. And he sware unto her, Whatsoever thou shalt ask of me, I will give it thee, unto the half of my kingdom. And she went forth, and said unto her mother, What shall I ask? And she said, The head of John the Baptist. **Mark 6:22-24**

Imagine being this young woman. Your uncle is now your stepfather and you are dancing to entertain this man, your mother's husband, and all his friends. Herod was clearly taken by her, offering up even half the kingdom. She takes him up on his offer. When she goes to her mother, to ask for advice. Her mother uses her as a pawn to get rid of the annoying critic of her illegal marriage, John the Baptist.

Whenever I read this passage, I wonder what did this dancing girl want? Did she enjoying entertaining these men? Did she want freedom from this life? Why didn't she speak up? Herod gave her an opportunity to say what she wanted and she didn't take it. At first glance, it's easy to judge the girl. It's easy to dismiss her as weak. But if we dig deeper into this scripture, it appears that she is just trapped. This girl was trapped in a mixed- up family. Her uncle/step-father was a murderous, selfish king and her mother was just like him. And she was stuck in the middle. Do you know anyone that seems trapped? Maybe we have a family member or a friend who seems trapped in a marriage with a selfish person. We think to ourselves, why doesn't she leave? Doesn't she want freedom? Why doesn't she speak up? But those questions aren't always fruitful. We don't know what is always going on in that household. Instead of judging wives in difficult situations, take some time to lift them up in prayer today. Think about a wife in your life that seems trapped. Ask God to give you wisdom on how to be a support and way of escape for her.

COFFEE WITH GOD

DAY TWENTY-FOUR

There was a prophetess, Anna, from the family of Phaneul in the tribe of Asher. Anna was very old. She had once been married for seven years. Then her husband dies, and she was a widow for eighty-four years. Anna never left the Temple but worshiped God, going without food and praying day and night. Luke 2:26 -38

If you continue reading on in this passage, you will see that Anna walks into the Temple right when Mary and Joseph are there with baby Jesus. We don't know how old Anna is but she was married for seven years and then a widow for eighty-four. She must be at least 100 years old. The scripture tells us that she did not remarry after her husband died. She was devoted to the temple and worshiping God. What a commitment!

Death is an extremely difficult experience, especially the death of a spouse. How we react to difficult experiences usually reveal the depth of our character. Anna must have been young when her husband died. His death did not separate her from her first love. She was faithful in her service, praying and fasting regularly. This faithfulness to God caused Anna to experience something much more fulfilling than a husband. Because of her commitment to service in the temple, she was able to encounter the Messiah. As a prophetess, I am sure she spoke to many people saying that a Messiah was coming. She was able to witness the personification of the prophesies of old, Christ in the flesh. In that moment, her many years of service and many long years of waiting met destiny. It was a divine appointment.

Being married is a great honor and joy, but it cannot be our only joy, our only commitment. We must be committed to Christ first. When we have Christ first in our lives, it enables us to encounter difficult circumstances with grace and assurance. We are inspired to go deeper in our relationship in Him in those times and the fruit of that is walking in purpose and destiny. Sometimes the wait is long. It is not always easy. But the fruit is worth it.

How would you define your commitment to Christ? How do you know that He is first in your life? In what ways can you be more committed to Him?

_____
_____
_____
_____
_____
_____
_____
_____
_____
_____
_____
_____
_____
_____
_____
_____
_____
_____

COFFEE WITH GOD

DAY TWENTY-FIVE

Jesus said, " Move the stone away." Martha, the sister of the dead man, said, "But Lord, it has been four days since he died. There will be a bad smell" John 11: 39

Martha was indeed a worrier and a work-a-holic. When her brother died, she blamed Jesus. She told him it wouldn't have happened if he would have been there.

How many times do we blame God when things don't go our way? She was so concerned about the "right now" that she had no time to sit back and see that God was using Lazarus' death for his glory. And of all things, when Jesus finally comes and tells her to move the stone, she tells him that if they move the stone, there will be a stench. Did Martha really care more about the smell than her brother? I doubt it. It was not that she didn't want her brother to be made alive again. She just didn't believe that Jesus would raise him from the dead. She was irritated at his weird request because she lacked faith.

I have often had a "Martha" spirit; so concerned with "works" that I missed the glory of God. As wives, it is so easy to get consumed with work, inside and outside of the house. It sometimes seems like the world will crumble without us and we can't seem to pull away from these responsibilities for an encounter. The problem with this perspective is that we can be so caught up in "doing" that we miss "experiencing". Martha was so preoccupied with her doubt that she was in the middle of a miracle and didn't even know it.

Has God ever given you a direction that does not make

"natural" sense? What is he saying to you now? How will you respond?

COFFEE WITH GOD

DAY TWENTY-SIX

She kept this up for many days. This bothered Paul, so he turned and said to the spirit, "By the power of Jesus Christ, I command you to come out of her!" Immediately, the spirit came out. When the owners of the servant girl saw this, they knew that now they could not use her to make money. So they grabbed Paul and Silas and dragged them before the city rulers in the marketplace. Acts 16:18-19

This scripture is interesting. We don't know much about this servant girl. We know that she was troubled by an evil spirit. This evil spirit caused her to tell the future and her owners used her trouble to make money. This girl was made to go places and make money for men that held her captive. She was bound by a spirit and needed freedom. Had she walked through that marketplace and not said anything, she would have continued in her turmoil. But God had different plans for her that day.

She saw Paul and Silas and followed them yelling behind them. Paul turned to her and commanded the spirit to come out. And it did. She was made free. God used the thing that kept her bound for years to provoke her deliverance. God is good to us in that way.

Today's devotion is not about you as a mom or a wife. It's about you as a daughter of God. What is your testimony? What is the thing that kept you bound for years? What is the thing that Satan wants to use to keep you from freedom? In what ways has God used that thing to provoke your deliverance or the deliverance of others?

COFFEE WITH GOD

DAY TWENTY-SEVEN

But clothe yourselves with the Lord Jesus Christ and forget about satisfying your sinful self Romans 13: 14

"Facebook is the devil!" I heard a women proclaim this over and over again as her reason for not joining the social media network. This caused me to ponder. Facebook is just a medium used by many people for many different things. If you use it to brag, lie, cheat, then it is easy to see why it can be easily identified as a tool of the devil. If you use it to connect with people, as another means for ministry, then not so much.

The one thing Facebook does offer is a window into the lives of others. Now, Facebook is not always a real look. Everyone chooses what they put in this window. Sometimes when we look at others' lives via Facebook or even through real life, there comes a temptation to compare, to envy, to covet.

Envy is a sin that robs women of genuine relationships. It is a tool that the enemy can use to cause us not to minister to our sister. The Word tells us to clothe ourselves with Jesus Christ, no other fashion trends matter. And we are to forget about satisfying ourselves.

When we live our lives in competition , then we are only satisfying our sinful flesh. God gets no glory from this and we become inefficient in our purpose. God alone has the blueprint for our lives. If we look anywhere else, we shift the focus from pleasing Him to pleasing others or ourselves. Where have you been tempted to compare your life? What areas are a struggle for you? Who do you find yourself in competition with?

How can you change that?

COFFEE WITH GOD

DAY TWENTY-EIGHT

Love patiently accepts all things. It always trusts, always hopes, and always remains strong.   *I Corinthians 13:7*

Love is not weak. The thirteenth chapter of I Corinthians is famously known as the "love" chapter. This chapter uses many action words to describe love. Love acts. Love is not passive. It is not a feeling. It is not an emotion. It is action.

I had a conversation once with a co-worker about someone who asked if it was possible to "fall out of love". For her, love was passive, something to fall in and out of. That is a dangerous way to view love, especially when you are married. Emotions come and go. Butterflies don't remain in the stomach forever. Love is a choice. It is a choice we make with every action. When we marry, we commit to love for a lifetime. Our vows aren't based on emotions. To have and hold forever, in sickness, and health, for richer and poorer takes incredible strength. Emotions are not bad. God gives them to us but they can be fleeting and misleading. We aren't to measure our love for our spouse, our covenant before God with things as fickle as emotions.

What are ways that you love your spouse? In what ways can you be even more intentional about showing love to your husband? And your children?

_____
_____
_____
_____
_____

COFFEE WITH GOD

DAY TWENTY-NINE

But he said to me, "My grace is enough for you. When you are weak, my power is made perfect in you." II Corinthians 12:9

There is no perfect wife. You will make mistakes. There will be times when you will fail as a wife and mom. God does not require us to be perfect. That is impossible. God requires us to be wives that love and trust in Him. That is it. Nothing more. Nothing less. Sometimes we will lose our temper with our husbands and children. We will spend too much money at the mall. We will work late hours. We will miss important events with our children. We will have messy houses. We will swear. We will sin. We will miss the mark. Our humanity makes these things inevitable. Accepting this as reality will make life a bit less stressful.

Accepting Christ's promise to be strong in our weakness makes it all the better. More than "accepting" our issues, He is welcoming our weaknesses. His grace is enough for all of our mess ups. God is not surprised when we get "out of control". He is waiting for us to get "out of control", so He can step in and do what He does best. Let Him have control. God's grace is enough for you. Today, take some time and rest in His grace. Let his strength be made perfect in your weakness.

_____
_____
_____
_____
_____

COFFEE WITH GOD

DAY THIRTY

Wives, yield to your husbands, as you do to the Lord. **Ephesians 5:22**

How are we to submit to the Lord? When God gives a direction, do we question it? Or better, *should* we question it? Is not God all knowing, all powerful? He created the world and everything in it. He knows the end of a thing at the beginning. Surely, we ought to submit to him fully. And in that same way we are to submit to our husbands. Submission trusts your husband's leadership. Because our husbands are human, it is so tempting to not follow this scripture completely.

I have been guilty of this. It's always easier to submit to him when I agree with what he is saying. But what about when I don't agree? The scripture doesn't tell us to only submit when we agree. This is the hardest part of submission, but it is the part that yields the greatest return. When we willingly submit to our husbands when we don't agree, we create a powerful force that is hard to break. It gives the husband relief because he feels strengthened and it sends a message to the enemy that "we are a team, no matter what".

In what areas is this difficult? Why? In what areas do you need to show the enemy that you are a team, no matter what? What are some practical ways that you can walk this out?

_____
_____
_____
_____
_____

COFFEE WITH GOD

DAY THIRTY-ONE

In the same way teach older women to be holy in their behavior, not speaking against others or enslaved to too much wine, but teaching what is good. Then they can teach the young women to love their husbands, to love their children, to be wise and pure, to be good workers at home, to be kind, and to yield to their husbands. Titus 2:3-5

We are not called to this life to be alone. It is great if your husband is your best friend. But he shouldn't be your only friend. We need each other. We need friends to encourage us and keep us sane. We need mentors to inspire us to grow and hold us accountable. We also need to mentor others, not so that we can tell other women what to do. We need to mentor so that we can help wives as they encounter struggles that we have encountered and overcome.

Often times, we may feel like we are alone on this journey. How refreshing to find other women on this journey with us. And even more refreshing to find someone that has been through the battle we are currently facing. It's a blessing to encounter someone that has been to the other side and can let us know – we can do it. As much as we need that, we need to also BE that for someone else. Take some time and pray about the women in your life. Who are your friends? Who are your mentors? Who are you mentoring? What can you do to improve these relationships?

_____
_____
_____

COFFEE WITH GOD

Please use the remainder of this journal to continue have your devotionals with God.

COFFEE WITH GOD

COFFEE WITH GOD

COFFEE WITH GOD

COFFEE WITH GOD

COFFEE WITH GOD

ABOUT THE AUTHOR

Charity R. Dean's mission is to serve God and serve others. She fulfills this through a commitment to civic engagement and serving her community. Charity has spent over a decade working with youth as a youth leader and mentor. In addition to youth, she is passionate about helping women walk in purpose and destiny. A lifelong Detroiter, Charity also is committed to helping her city thrive in any way she can.

Charity lives in the city she loves with her wonderfully supportive and patient husband Erik, her comedic son, Elijah and her compassionate daughter, Lauren. To learn more about the author or to connect with her directly, please visit www.charityrdean.com.

www.ingramcontent.com/pod-product-compliance
Lightning Source LLC
Chambersburg PA
CBHW071659040426
42446CB00011B/1836